The Power of a
PRAYING®
LIFE

Prayer and Study Guide

STORMIE
OMARTIAN

HARVEST HOUSE PUBLISHERS

EUGENE, OREGON

THE POWER OF A PRAYING® LIFE PRAYER AND STUDY GUIDE
Copyright © 2010 by Stormie Omartian
Published by Harvest House Publishers
Eugene, Oregon 97402
www.harvesthousepublishers.com

ISBN 978-0-7369-2691-1

This book belongs to

_____

Please do not read beyond this page
without permission of the person named above.

———

A supplemental workbook to

The Power of a Praying® Life

by Stormie Omartian
for anyone interested in
practical group or individual study.

———

Contents

WHAT YOU SHOULD
KNOW BEFORE YOU BEGIN

Welcome to the process of living a praying life. And it *is* a process. It doesn't happen overnight, but it *does* happen a little every day as you grow in your relationship with the Lord and follow His leading.

This PRAYER AND STUDY GUIDE is designed to help you develop unwavering faith, a greater knowledge of God and His ways, and a closer step-by-step walk with Him. By responding to the questions and suggestions for each chapter, you will increase your understanding of God's Word and learn the many ways you can pray in power according to His will in order to effect positive change in your life.

What You Need to Have

This is a 30-week plan—or a 30-*day* plan for those of you who have the time and want to move quickly. Or you can simply go at your own pace and do *whatever* you can, *whenever* you want. However you choose to proceed, remember that consistent effort will reap great rewards for you.

In order to complete this PRAYER AND STUDY GUIDE, you need to have my book THE POWER OF A PRAYING LIFE (from now on referred to as "the book") and your own Bible. I have used the New King James Version here, but you can use whatever translation speaks to your heart.

You will also find it beneficial to have a small notebook or journal with you so you can write down whatever God reveals to you about yourself, your life, and your relationship and walk with Him. My hope is that there will not be enough room in this book to contain all that God reveals to you. (And don't forget a pen or pencil.)

If You Are Doing This in a Group

When doing this as a group study, read the chapter assigned that week from the book and then answer the corresponding questions in this PRAYER AND STUDY GUIDE. When the group meets together, the leader will go over the questions and encourage members of the group to share the answers or insights they have received from the Lord while doing the study. Because some of the questions are personal, you don't need to say anything you are not comfortable sharing with the group. At the same time, feel free to be transparent and candid about your own personal experience whenever you feel led by the Spirit to do so. Your freedom to share can release others who are hesitant or fearful, and great personal growth for everyone can come from that.

The answers to Bible-based questions are *always* good to share with one another, however, so don't hesitate to contribute in that way. There will be things you have learned, discovered, or experienced that will be beneficial for others to hear. For example, you could explain how a Scripture spoke to you or enlightened your mind or changed your attitude, and that can be very enriching for the other members of the group.

I suggest praying the prayer together at the end of each chapter in the book and letting that be the starting point of a prayer time where people are led to pray as needed about the things that concern them.

The leader should always be aware of the clock so that the group begins and ends on time. Most people are overloaded with obligations and schedules and simply cannot be in a group that runs way beyond the predetermined time. The result of group meetings that consistently go too long will be that people stop coming.

Ask God to Change Your Life

In this PRAYER AND STUDY GUIDE, you will often be asked to write out your prayers. Just as spoken prayers are powerful, so are the prayers you write from your heart. These written prayers will not only help you focus on what to pray about, but they will also help you to develop a richer prayer life with the Lord. You will become more and more comfortable communicating with Him. It is my prayer that God will speak to you and change your life in a wonderful way through this PRAYER AND STUDY GUIDE, and you will be walking so close to Him that you will find your life working the way it should.

WEEK ONE

Read the Introduction: "How Can I Make My Life Work"
and Chapter 1: "Know Who Your Father Is" in THE POWER
OF A PRAYING LIFE (This will be the longest reading
assignment in the PRAYER AND STUDY GUIDE, but it will
lay the foundation you need for the rest of the study.)

1. In light of the section titled "What Is True Success?" on pages 8-10
    in the book, how would you briefly describe what true success in
    life is?

    _____

    _____

    _____

    _____

    _____

    Is what you wrote above different in any way from what you previ-
    ously thought of as success? Ask God to show you if you are not
    sure. Write out your answer as a prayer. (For example, "Lord, show
    me any way I have an attitude about what success is that is not in

line with Your ways. Help me to understand that true success is not in how much I have or what I accomplish, but rather...")

_____

_____

_____

_____

_____

2. In the section titled "Knowing What Your True Needs Are" on pages 11-13 in the book, which of the needs listed do you most want met? Because we each need all of them, list the top five that are most important to you right now.

1. _____

_____

2. _____

_____

3. _____

_____

4. _____

_____

5. _____

_____

3. Read 2 Corinthians 6:14-18. What are the conditions we must meet (verse 17) in order for God to be a father to us?

_____

_____

_____

_____

4. Read John 1:12-13. What is the condition you must meet in order to be a child of God?

_____

_____

5. Read Jeremiah 9:3. What reasons did God give for the fact that His people did evil?

_____

_____

6. Read the following Scriptures, and next to each one write what those verses speak to you about God and how they help you to know Him better.

Isaiah 12:2-3 _____

_____

_____

Psalm 34:15-16 _____

_____

_____

Psalm 16:7-8 _____

_____

_____

Psalm 18:1-2 _____

_____

_____

7. How would you describe the relationship you have with your earthly father?

_____

_____

_____

_____

8. Do you see any way—either negatively or positively—that your relationship with your earthly father may have affected your relationship with your heavenly Father? Explain. (For example, "My father was distant and not affectionate, so I tend to think of God as being distant as well.")

_____

_____

_____

_____

9. Read Matthew 6:26-30. What do these verses speak to you about how your Father God loves you?

_____

_____

_____

_____

10. Read Matthew 6:31-32. What do these verses speak to you about how God thinks of you?

_____

_____

_____

11. Read Matthew 7:8-11. What do these verses speak to you about the goodness of your heavenly Father toward you?

_____

_____

_____

_____

_____

12. Pray out loud the prayer on pages 22-23 in the book. Then choose one of the Scriptures in the Word Power section on pages 23-24 and write it out below as a prayer. (For example, "Thank You, Father God, that You love me enough to call me Your child…")

_____

_____

_____

_____

Week Two

Read Chapter 2: "Receive All That Jesus Died for
You to Have" in The Power of a Praying Life

1. Read John 10:9. Have you walked through the door of salvation
    by receiving Jesus as your Savior? Have you found the rest, provi-
    sion, and sustenance in the peaceful pasture He has for you? If so,
    describe your experience. If not, describe how you feel about that.
    Do you sense a need for that profound connection with God?

    _____

    _____

    _____

    _____

    _____

2. Read Romans 3:23-26. Who needs salvation and why?

    _____

    _____

    _____

_____

_____

3. Read Romans 5:18-21. These verses are talking about Adam's disobedience and the obedience of Jesus. What happened as a result
   of Adam's disobedience?

   _____

   _____

   _____

   What happened as a result of Jesus' obedience?

   _____

   _____

   _____

4. Read the following Scriptures and explain what Jesus accomplished
   for you.

   Revelation 1:5-6 _____

   _____

   _____

   John 4:14 _____

   _____

   _____

   Romans 5:9-10 _____

   _____

   _____

Titus 2:14 _____

_____

_____

5. Read 1 Corinthians 1:18-21. According to these verses, what is the message of the cross to those who are lost in their sins?

    _____

    _____

    What is the message of the cross to those who receive Jesus?

    _____

    _____

    What does God say about the wisdom of the world?

    _____

    _____

6. Read Philippians 2:9-11. These verses are talking about Jesus. What do they say about the name of Jesus?

    _____

    _____

    _____

7. Read Matthew 10:32-33. What happens when we speak to others about our faith, openly sharing that we have received Jesus?

    _____

_____

_____

What happens when we hide the fact that we have received Jesus?

_____

_____

_____

8. Read the following Scriptures and write down the characteristics, description, or names of Jesus expressed in each one.

Isaiah 59:20 _____

_____

_____

Psalm 16:2 _____

_____

_____

Isaiah 9:6 _____

_____

_____

Read the section titled "Because of Jesus in You" on pages 28-31 in the book. Which three of the benefits of receiving Jesus do you most tend to forget in your own life? Write them out as a prayer. (For example, "Lord, help me to remember that because of You I don't have to live in guilt...")

1. _____

_____

2. _____
_____
_____

3. _____
_____
_____

9. Read Romans 10:13 and John 6:37. Think of people you care about who do not yet know the Lord. None of us ever wants to grieve over the loss of a loved one who we fear did not know the Lord. We don't know if, in the moment before death, that loved one didn't cry out to Jesus. Even if he or she was in a coma or killed in an accident, instant recognition of Jesus as Lord and crying out to Him is still possible. Only God knows who has called out to Him with a sincere heart of longing to be with Him and who has not. Jesus does not want anyone to perish without knowing Him. Write out a prayer for the people you know who need salvation, naming them before the Lord and praying that they will call on the name of Jesus. Thank Jesus that He will never turn away anyone who comes to Him.

_____
_____
_____
_____
_____

10. Pray out loud the prayer on pages 33-34 in the book. Then choose one of the Scriptures in the Word Power section on pages 34-35

and write it out below as a prayer. (For example, "Lord, I thank You that You have prepared a place for me in Your kingdom...")

_____

_____

_____

_____

_____

→ ←

WEEK THREE

Read Chapter 3: "Welcome the Holy Spirit's Presence" in THE POWER OF A PRAYING LIFE

1. Of the nine items listed under "What Having the Holy Spirit Means for You" in this chapter—each of which is crucial for your life—choose the one that means the most to you at this time and explain why that is.

_____

_____

_____

_____

_____

2. Of those same nine items listed in "What Having the Holy Spirit Means for You," which one do you most need to be reminded of today? Why?

_____

_____

_____

_____

_____

3.   Read Galatians 3:2 and answer Paul's question as if he were asking it of you.

_____

_____

4.   Read Romans 8:27 and 1 Corinthians 12:11. Write out the Scripture and reference below each statement that best supports it.

The Holy Spirit has a mind.

_____

_____

_____

_____

The Holy Spirit has a will.

_____

_____

_____

_____

5.   Read Matthew 12:31-32. How serious is it to speak blasphemy against the Holy Spirit? Why do you think that is?

_____

_____

_____

_____

Read Ephesians 4:30-31. What are some of the things a person could do that you believe would grieve the Holy Spirit?

_____

_____

_____

_____

_____

6. Read Genesis 41:38, 1 Samuel 16:13, and Daniel 4:9. These Scriptures speak of Joseph, David, and Daniel, respectively. What was the common trait of all three of these men?

_____

_____

How important do you believe this common trait was in the greatness of their achievements?

_____

_____

_____

How important do you believe this same trait is for you and your ability to do great things for God in your own life? Why?

_____

_____

_____

_____

7. Read the Scriptures below. On the line below, write one of the following descriptions of the Holy Spirit supported by those Scriptures:

> The Holy Spirit is omniscient (all-knowing)
>
> The Holy Spirit is omnipresent (always with you)
>
> The Holy Spirit is omnipotent (all-powerful)
>
> The Holy Spirit is eternal (always exists)

"How much more shall the blood of Christ, who through the eternal Spirit offered Himself without spot to God, cleanse your conscience from dead works to serve the living God?" (Hebrews 9:14).

_____

"Where can I go from Your Spirit? Or where can I flee from Your presence? If I ascend into heaven, You are there; if I make my bed in hell, behold, You are there. If I take the wings of the morning, and dwell in the uttermost parts of the sea, even there Your hand shall lead me, and Your right hand shall hold me" (Psalm 139:7-10).

_____

"And the angel answered and said to her, 'The Holy Spirit will come upon you, and the power of the Highest will overshadow you; therefore, also, that Holy One who is to be born will be called the Son of God'" (Luke 1:35).

_____

"God has revealed them to us through His Spirit. For the Spirit searches all things, yes, the deep things of God. For what man knows the things of a man except the spirit of the man which is in him? Even so no one knows the things of God except the Spirit of God" (1 Corinthians 2:10-11).

_____

8. Read Romans 8:5-8. In light of these verses, why is it important to be led by the Spirit in all you do?

_____

_____

_____

_____

_____

9. According to the following Scriptures, what does the Holy Spirit do for us?

2 Peter 1:21 _____

_____

_____

John 14:26 _____

_____

_____

Romans 15:13 _____

_____

_____

Romans 8:1 _____

_____

_____

John 15:26 _____

_____

_____

10. Pray out loud the prayer on pages 41-42 in the book. Then choose one of the Scriptures in the Word Power section on pages 42-43 and write it out below as a prayer. (For example, "Lord, thank You that Your Spirit is within me. Cause me to walk in Your ways...")

_____

_____

_____

_____

_____

→ ←

Week Four

Read Chapter 4: "Take God at His Word"
in The Power of a Praying Life

1. Read the section titled "A Few Good Reasons to Let God's Word Live in You" on pages 47-48 in the book. Though acknowledging that every reason listed is crucial to your life, which of the reasons listed do you most want to come alive in your heart today? Explain your answer. (For example, "I want Proverbs 28:9 to come alive in my heart today because I never want to ignore God's laws in any way and as a result keep my prayers from being heard.")

_____

_____

_____

_____

_____

2. Read the Scriptures below and write a short prayer inspired by each Scripture. (For example, Proverbs 28:9: "Lord, help me to hear and understand Your law so that my prayers are always acceptable to You...") All of these Scriptures are listed on pages 47-48 in the

book so you don't have to look them up in your Bible unless you want to underline them.

Proverbs 28:9 _____

_____

John 15:7 _____

_____

Proverbs 10:25 _____

_____

Psalm 107:20 _____

_____

Proverbs 12:28 _____

_____

Psalm 84:11 _____

_____

Psalm 119:165 _____

_____

Joshua 1:8 _____

_____

Matthew 4:4 _____

_____

Psalm 15:1-2 _____

_____

3. Read the following Scriptures in your Bible. Next to each one, write down what it is that you gain from God's Word.

Matthew 7:24 _____

_____

1 Peter 2:2 _____

_____

Psalm 119:28 _____

_____

Psalm 119:114 _____

_____

Psalm 119:130 _____

_____

4. Read Romans 10:17. How do we increase our faith in God?

_____

_____

5. Read John 1:1-5 and John 1:14. Who is being referred to as the Word in these Scriptures? What do these Scriptures speak to you about who Jesus is?

_____

_____

_____

6. Read Psalm 119:50 and Psalm 119:105. In light of these verses, what does God's Word mean to you?

_____

_____

_____

_____

_____

7. Read Psalm 119:101-102. What do you have to do in order to live God's way?

_____

_____

_____

_____

_____

8. What do the following Scriptures say to you about God's Word? In light of each one, how important and exalted is the Word of God? (These Scriptures can be found on page 51 of the book.)

Isaiah 40:8 _____

_____

Psalm 138:2 _____

_____

Luke 21:33 _____

_____

9. Read Hebrews 4:12 and Psalm 1:1-3 in your Bible or on page 51 of the book. What are the specific things mentioned in these verses that assure you of what God's Word will do for you and your life?

_____

_____

_____

_____

_____

_____

10. Pray out loud the prayer on page 50 in the book. Then choose one of the Scriptures in the Word Power section on page 51 and write it out as a prayer. (For example, "Thank You, Lord, that Your Word is alive and it is powerful, and it is…")

_____

_____

_____

_____

_____

→ ←

Week Five

Read Chapter 5: "Make Worship a Habit" in
The Power of a Praying Life

1. Read Hebrews 13:15 and Psalm 34:1-2. How often are we supposed to give God worship and praise?

_____

_____

How often do you give praise to God? In what ways would you
like to improve on that?

_____

_____

_____

_____

2. Read 1 Peter 2:9. Why have you been chosen to be a part of a royal
priesthood and a special people?

_____

_____

_____

3. Read the following Scriptures. Next to each one write a prayer of
    praise to God inspired by that verse or verses. (For example, "Lord,
    I praise You for Your mercy to me and that it is…")

    Psalm 103:17-18 _____

    _____

    _____

    Psalm 106:1 _____

    _____

    _____

    Genesis 1:27-28 _____

    _____

    _____

    John 3:16 _____

    _____

    _____

    Psalm 107:8 _____

    _____

    _____

    Titus 3:4-7 _____

    _____

    _____

4. Read Isaiah 40:28-31. Write out a prayer of praise to God for the special blessings from God mentioned in these verses.

_____

_____

_____

_____

_____

5. Read Psalm 103:1-12 (or you can find it in the section titled "When You Want to Be Inspired to Worship" on pages 55-56 in the book. Write out a prayer of praise to God for all of His blessings that are mentioned in these verses.

_____

_____

_____

_____

_____

6. Read the following Scriptures in your Bible. Write out a prayer of praise for all that specifically inspires thanksgiving to God in your heart in each verse.

1 Corinthians 6:14 _____

_____

2 Corinthians 13:4 _____

_____

Romans 5:8-9 _____

_____

7. Read Psalm 139:13-16. Write out a prayer thanking God for all that inspires praise in these verses. Include in your prayer the things about *you* for which you are thankful. This is not an exercise in pride or self-focus. It is right to recognize the Giver of Life as the source of all that is good about the way He made you.

_____

_____

_____

_____

_____

8. Read Psalm 92:1-2 and Psalm 145:2-3. When is a good time to praise God?

_____

_____

_____

9. Write out a prayer of worship and praise for all the ways you are thankful to God for your life.

_____

_____

_____

_____

_____

_____

Are you able to praise God even in difficult and painful times? If you answered yes, explain how you are able to do that. If you answered no, write out a prayer asking God to help you make praise your first reaction to whatever happens.

_____

_____

_____

_____

10. Pray out loud the prayer on pages 57-58 in the book. Then choose a Scripture in the Word Power section on pages 58-59 and write it out as a prayer. (For example, "Lord, help me to bless You at all times...")

_____

_____

_____

_____

_____

➤ ⬥

Week Six

Read Chapter 6: "Pray As Though Your Life
Depends on It" in THE POWER OF A PRAYING LIFE

1. In the section titled "Resisting the Temptation to Not Pray" on pages 63-64 in the book, are there any reasons listed there that have kept you from praying as much as you should? Everyone has some struggle with prayer. What keeps you from praying as much as you would like to pray or feel you should pray? (For example, "I have sometimes felt that I am not good enough to deserve an answer to prayer, and I know that has kept me from praying as much as I should.")

   _____

   _____

   _____

   _____

2. Read the section titled "What Jesus Said About Prayer" on page 65. In your own words, write what His words mean to you regarding your prayer life.

   _____

_____

_____

_____

3. Read Luke 11:5-8. Jesus is speaking here about prayer. What do His words speak to you about your own prayers?

_____

_____

_____

_____

4. Read Jeremiah 33:3, Psalm 138:3, Psalm 50:15, and Jeremiah 29:12-13. Write out the Scripture and reference below the heading that best describes that particular benefit of prayers.

To have God hear your prayer

_____

_____

_____

To find God's help in difficult times

_____

_____

_____

To see God answer your prayer

_____

_____

_____

_____

To gain new understanding from God

_____

_____

_____

_____

5. Read Mark 6:5-6. These verses are talking about when Jesus visited Nazareth and tried to do miracles there. Why couldn't Jesus do a mighty work in Nazareth? What does that mean for you as far as seeing God do a mighty work in response to *your* prayers?

_____

_____

_____

_____

If *Jesus* could not do a miracle in the presence of unbelief, what could your own unbelief do?

_____

_____

Can you think of a time when your own doubt may have cost you an answer to your prayers? Explain.

_____

_____

_____

_____

_____

6. Read the following Scriptures and describe in your own words how you should pray.

Luke 18:1 _____

_____

1 Thessalonians 5:17 _____

_____

James 5:16 _____

_____

7. Read 1 John 3:22. What does this Scripture speak to you about the connection between obedience to God's ways and prayer?

_____

_____

_____

_____

_____

8. Read Ephesians 6:17-18. These two verses describe part of the

armor of God. How are you supposed to pray in order to arm yourself and do spiritual warfare?

_____

_____

_____

_____

9. Read John 16:23-24 and John 15:14-16. Jesus was speaking to His disciples here about prayer. With regard to praying, what do these two sections of Scripture have in common? How is He telling you to pray?

_____

_____

_____

10. Pray out loud the prayer on pages 67-68 in the book. Then choose one of the Scriptures in the Word Power section on page 68 and write it out below as a prayer. (For example, "Lord, I cry out to You in the midst of all that troubles me, and I thank You that You will…")

_____

_____

_____

_____

_____

> ⇥ ⇤

Week Seven

Read Chapter 7: "Live in the Freedom God Has for You" in The Power of a Praying Life

1. Read the following Scriptures. Next to each one, tell where deliverance is found.

   Psalm 22:4-5 _____

   _____

   Proverbs 21:31_____

   _____

   Psalm 56:12-13 _____

   _____

2. Read 2 Corinthians 1:9-10. What is the hope in these verses for you?

   _____

   _____

   _____

   Is there anything in your life you would especially like to be set free from that you feel may require ongoing deliverance in the future? For example, are there certain habits of thought or action that have been a recurring problem or annoyance to you? Write out your answer as a prayer and thank God that He will *continue* to deliver you.

_____

_____

_____

_____

3. Read Luke 4:18-21. Jesus is speaking to people in the synagogue, and He is reading from the book of Isaiah (Isaiah 61:1-2). Jesus then told the people those verses were now fulfilled. In other words, that section of Scripture in Isaiah 61 was talking about Him, and He was there to fulfill it. According to these verses, what did Jesus come to do for you personally?

_____

_____

_____

_____

4. Read Romans 7:21-25. What is bringing Paul into captivity?

_____

_____

_____

Who can deliver him from this?

_____

_____

In light of that, who can deliver you from any captivity you may ever have to sin?

_____

_____

5. Is there any area of your life where you feel trapped by wrong thoughts or actions? Do you ever want to do the right thing but end up doing the wrong thing? If so, write out a prayer asking Jesus to strengthen you and set you free from all that. If you answered no, then write out a prayer asking God to show you any place in your life where you need greater release or freedom.

_____

_____

_____

_____

_____

6. Read Romans 11:26-27. This passage is foretelling the coming of Jesus.

What was Jesus referred to as?

_____

What was predicted would happen when Jesus came to earth?

_____

_____

_____

_____

7. Read Galatians 5:1. In this Scripture, Paul is talking about standing firm in the liberty we have because of Jesus and not becoming a slave to it again. Jesus set us free from slavery to sin, and He wants us to remain free. Do you believe you can stand strong in the freedom from sin Christ has given you? Are you able to keep from falling back into anything from which you have been set free? Write out your answers as a prayer, asking God to help you stand strong in the freedom He has given you and will give you in the future.

    _____

    _____

    _____

    _____

    _____

8. Read 2 Timothy 4:16-18. Paul was abandoned by some when he went before the court. But who did *not* abandon him? What did the Lord do for him? What was the Lord *going* to do for him?

    _____

    _____

    _____

    _____

    _____

9. Write out a prayer of praise and thanksgiving to God that He will deliver you from every evil work. Name any specific evil work you want to be delivered from in your life right now. By evil work, I mean anything that you know is not of the Lord and that goes

against His will for you. (For example, doubt, fear, enemy attacks, bad influences, etc.)

_____

_____

_____

_____

_____

10. Pray out loud the prayer on pages 73-74 in the book. Then choose one of the Scriptures in the Word Power section on pages 74-75 and write it out as a prayer. (For example, "Lord, help me to stand fast in the liberty by which You have…")

_____

_____

_____

_____

_____

WEEK EIGHT

Read Chapter 8: "Seek God's Kingdom and
His Gifts" in THE POWER OF A PRAYING LIFE

1. Read the following Scriptures. Write down what each one says
about the kingdom of God.

Mark 12:32-34 _____

_____

_____

Luke 9:62 _____

_____

_____

John 3:5 _____

_____

_____

John 18:36 _____

_____

_____

Romans 14:17 _____

_____

_____

1 Corinthians 15:22-24 _____

_____

_____

Hebrews 12:28 _____

_____

_____

2 Peter 1:10-11 _____

_____

_____

2. Read Romans 5:17-18. Reference to "one man's offense" is talking
    about Adam. "One Man's righteous act" is referring to Jesus. What
    is the free gift of God given to us because of what Jesus did?

    _____

    _____

    _____

3. Read the following Scriptures. Write down what gift from God is
    referred to in each verse.

    John 14:27 _____

    _____

    Romans 6:23: _____

    _____

4. Read 1 Corinthians 6:11. In this verse, "washed" means to be cleansed from all sin. "Sanctified" means to be set apart for God. And "justified" means to be totally accepted by the Lord, because it is just as if you've never sinned. Write out a prayer thanking God for these specific life-changing gifts from Him.

_____

_____

_____

_____

5. Read the following Scriptures. Write down what you must do to enter the kingdom of God.

John 3:3 _____

_____

Matthew 3:2 _____

_____

Matthew 19:24_____

_____

Matthew 18:1-4 _____

_____

6. Read James 1:17. Where do all good gifts come from?

_____

_____

What are some of the gifts you have received from God?

_____

_____

_____

_____

7. Read Matthew 7:11. When you want to receive gifts from God, what should you do?

_____

_____

Write out a prayer asking God to give you the gifts you most desire right now. (For example, "Lord, I ask You for gifts of Your love, mercy, power, peace…")

_____

_____

_____

_____

_____

8. Read Romans 8:38-39. The gift of God's love is one of the greatest of all His gifts to you. But even though these verses say that nothing can separate you from His love, there can still come times when you don't sense His love in your life. That happens when you take your eyes off of His truth and put them on your feelings and emotions. Write out a prayer praising God for His love toward you, and thanking Him that nothing can change that or separate you from it. Ask Him to enable you to trust His love for you at all times.

_____

_____

_____

_____

_____

9. Read Ephesians 2:8. Write out a prayer thanking God for His grace operating in your life to save you. Also include thanks for any other specific time you can remember when God did not give you the punishment or consequences you deserved.

_____

_____

_____

_____

_____

10. Pray out loud the prayer on page 81 in the book. Then choose one of the Scriptures in the Word Power section on pages 81-82 and write it out as a prayer. (For example, "Holy Spirit, help me to know the things that have been freely given to me by God…")

_____

_____

_____

_____

_____

WEEK NINE

Read Chapter 9: "Maintain a Right Heart"
in THE POWER OF A PRAYING LIFE

1. Read Ezekiel 18:31. In light of this Scripture, how could you get yourself a new heart and a new spirit?

_____

_____

_____

_____

2. Read 1 Corinthians 4:5 and Matthew 22:37-38. In light of these Scriptures, write out a prayer to God asking Him to show you what is in your heart. (For example "Lord, I pray You would reveal any darkness in my heart and…")

_____

_____

_____

_____

_____

3. Read Hebrews 12:5-6 and 12:11. It is a courageous and good thing when you submit your heart to God for cleansing, because He will surely show you attitudes that have to go. Why does He correct us? How are we supposed to react to His chastening? Even though it can be painful, what is the result?

    _____

    _____

    _____

    _____

    _____

4. Read Acts 15:8-9. Peter, who was a Jew, is talking about how God called him to preach the gospel to the Gentiles. What did God do for the Gentiles, and how did He purify their hearts?

    _____

    _____

    _____

5. Read the following Scriptures. Next to each reference, explain what the condition of your heart should be and how you achieve that.

    James 4:8 _____

    _____

    _____

    Ephesians 4:32 _____

    _____

    _____

    Deuteronomy 26:16 _____

_____

_____

Proverbs 3:5 _____

_____

_____

Ephesians 6:5-6 _____

_____

_____

1 Peter 1:22 _____

_____

_____

6. Read Psalm 27:14. What are you to do in order to see God do a work in your heart? What will God do in response?

_____

_____

7. How would you describe the condition of your heart right now? How would you like to see it improved? Write out your answer as a prayer to God. (For example, "Lord, I feel that there is hardness in my heart. I ask that You would fill my heart with…")

_____

_____

_____

_____

8. Read the following Scriptures, and then write out what the consequences are for having a hard heart. What might we forfeit if we allow our hearts to become or remain hard?

Proverbs 29:1 _____

_____

_____

Hebrews 3:8-11_____

_____

_____

Job 9:4 _____

_____

_____

9. Read the following Scriptures. Describe what can cause your heart to be hard.

Hebrews 3:12-13 _____

_____

Psalm 95:8 _____

_____

Read Deuteronomy 15:7-8. What did God want the people to do instead of hardening their hearts?

_____

_____

_____

Read the following Scriptures, and then answer the following question: What grieved Jesus?

Mark 3:5 _____

_____

Mark 16:14 _____

_____

Matthew 19:8 _____

_____

10. Pray out loud the prayer on pages 87-88 in the book. Then choose one of the Scriptures in the Word Power section on page 88 and write it out below as a prayer. (For example, "Lord, I pray You will help me to diligently guard my heart...")

_____

_____

_____

_____

_____

_____

→ ←

Week Ten

Read Chapter 10: "Move in Forgiveness—God's
and Yours" in The Power of a Praying Life

1. Read Psalm 103:12. Do you feel your sins of the past have been removed completely from you as described in this verse? Have you been able to receive God's full forgiveness? Write out your answer as a prayer to God. (For example, "Lord, I still feel guilty about what happened…" Or, "Lord, if there is any place in me where I have not fully received Your forgiveness, reveal that to me so that I can…")

_____

_____

_____

_____

_____

2. Read Proverbs 19:11. According to this Scripture, what are you to do when someone hurts you? Do you find it easy to do that?

_____

_____

_____

_____

3. Read Matthew 22:37-39. Next to loving God, what is the second most important thing you can do?

_____

_____

Write out a prayer asking God to help you love others as yourself. Tell Him you know this is too hard to do without His help.

_____

_____

_____

_____

4. Read the following Scriptures. What are these verses telling you to do?

Matthew 18:21-22 _____

_____

Matthew 18:32-35 _____

_____

Colossians 3:13 _____

_____

Is there anyone in your life whom you find difficult to forgive over and over? If so, write out a prayer asking God to help you forgive as the Bible says to forgive. If you cannot think of anyone you need to forgive, ask God to show you anything you are not seeing.

_____

_____

_____

_____

_____

5. Read Exodus 20:12, Luke 18:20, and Ephesians 6:2. What is the common message in each of these Scriptures?

_____

_____

The Bible says if you want to have a long life and be blessed, you must honor your father and mother. One of the best ways to give them honor is to be thankful for them. Think of the five top reasons you are thankful for your mother and father and complete the prayer below. Whether you can think of a thousand things or you are having a hard time thinking of anything, ask God to help you. The fact that you are alive today means they must have done something right.

"Lord, the ways I am most thankful for my father are…"

1 _____

2. _____

3. _____

4. _____

5. _____

"Lord, the ways I am most thankful for my mother are..."

1._____

2._____

3._____

4._____

5._____

Ask God to show you any unforgiveness you may have toward either of your parents. Even if your parents died when you were young, forgive them for that. Children sometimes think their parents could have done something to prevent their demise. This kind of thinking can become a barrier to your relationship with God. Complete the prayers below.

Lord, help me forgive my father for...

_____

_____

_____

_____

Lord, help me forgive my mother for...

_____

_____

_____

_____

Read Psalm 27:10. Without forgiving your parents, you will not be fully able to honor your father and mother. Once you forgive everything, you will begin to heal in your relationship to them, and you will better sense your heavenly Father's love for you. What does this Scripture speak personally to your heart?

_____

_____

_____

_____

6. Read the Scriptures below, and then answer the following questions. What are we supposed to do in our relationships with others? What happens when we don't do that?

    Hebrews 12:14-15 _____

    _____

    _____

    1 Peter 3:8-9 _____

    _____

    _____

7. Read Matthew 7:3-5. Is there anyone you feel critical of? Is that attitude robbing you of your peace? Write out a prayer asking God to take away any critical spirit you may have. Don't feel badly about that. A critical attitude can creep into any of us at any time. Also, ask God to make you aware of anything you do that could be irritating to others. Write down anything God reveals to you.

    _____

    _____

    _____

    _____

_____

_____

8. Read 1 John 2:11 and Romans 14:10. What are the consequences
    when we entertain resentment or judgmental thoughts toward
    another person?

_____

_____

_____

9. Read Philippians 2:1-2 and 1 Thessalonians 5:15. What are we
    supposed to do with the people God puts in our lives?

_____

_____

_____

_____

10. Pray out loud the prayer on pages 92-93 in the book. Then choose
    one of the Scriptures in the Word Power section on pages 93-94
    and write it out as a prayer below. (For example, "Lord, help me
    to not sit in judgment on others...")

_____

_____

_____

_____

→ ←

Week Eleven

Read Chapter 11: "Fear God, but Don't Live
in Fear" in The Power of a Praying Life

1. Read Psalm 86:11. When your heart becomes divided, you lose
   the fear of the Lord. That's why the psalmist asks God to unite his
   heart. In what ways could your heart be divided? How could those
   divisions be directed toward one focus? (For example, your heart
   could become divided if material things became more important
   than spiritual things, such as if your heart is drawn toward watch-
   ing television to the exclusion of reading the Word of God. This
   doesn't mean that television is bad, or that you must be legalistic
   about reading the Bible. It just means that when something *other*
   than God becomes more important than the *things* of God, we can
   lose the *fear* of God without ever intending to do so.)

   _____

   _____

   _____

   _____

   _____

2. Read the following Scriptures that are all about the fear of the Lord.

Beside each one, explain what advantage there is for you to have the fear of God.

Psalm 112:1-2 _____

_____

Psalm 112:3 _____

_____

Psalm 112:4 _____

_____

Psalm 112:6 _____

_____

Psalm 112:7 _____

_____

Psalm 112:8 _____

_____

3. Read Psalm 103:13 and Psalm 115:13. What does God do for those who reverence Him?

_____

_____

_____

_____

4. Read the first page of chapter 11 on page 95 in the book, and answer the following questions.

What does having the fear of God mean?

_____

_____

_____

What kind of people do not have the fear of God?

_____

_____

Where do wisdom and understanding come from?

_____

_____

5. Read the following Scriptures in your Bible or in the Word Power section on page 102 in the book. Beside each one, answer the following question: What does having the fear of the Lord do for you?

Proverbs 14:27 _____

_____

Proverbs 22:4 _____

_____

Psalm 103:17 _____

_____

6. Read Mark 4:39-40. When Jesus was talking to His disciples, who were afraid of the storm, what did He ask them?

_____

_____

Whenever you become afraid, what do you need to have?

_____

_____

_____

7. Read Isaiah 35:3-6. God wants us to have the fear of the Lord, but He does not want us to live in fear that He will forsake us or not provide for us. He wants us to trust Him. In your own words, describe what is promised to the people of God in these verses.

_____

_____

_____

_____

_____

These verses in Isaiah 35 speak of hopeless places in our own lives—being blind, deaf, lame, or needing water in the desert—and the promise that with God impossible things are now possible. You don't have to fear, because God will strengthen you when the things you face make you feel weak. Is there any place in your life where you feel fearful? For example, do you feel fearful in the area of finances, health, relationships, marriage, children, growing old, dying, or losing a loved one? Write out your answer to that question as a prayer. (For example, "Lord, I am afraid that financially I won't be able to keep my home…") Ask God to take away that fear and give you His peace.

_____

_____

_____

_____

_____

8. Look at the section titled "What Happens When You Have the Fear of God?" on pages 96-97 in the book. Keeping in mind that we need all of the advantages of fearing God listed there, choose two or three of the items and tell why they are important to you. (For example, "I am so grateful that the fear of God in me will keep my life from being shortened, and it will deliver me from...")

    _____

    _____

    _____

    _____

    _____

9. Read the following Scriptures in your Bible or on page 100 in the book. What will keep you from having ungodly fear?

    Psalm 23:4 _____

    _____

    _____

    Isaiah 41:10 _____

    _____

    _____

    1 John 4:18 _____

    _____

    _____

10. Pray out loud the prayer on pages 101-102 in the book. Then choose one of the Scriptures in the Word Power section on page 102 and write it out as a prayer. (For example, "Lord, I thank You

that even though You are almighty God, You are still my heavenly Father who has compassion on me…")

_____

_____

_____

_____

_____

Week Twelve

Read Chapter 12: "Replace Doubt with Unwavering Faith" in The Power of a Praying Life

1. Read Romans 12:3. Everyone has *some* faith. How would you describe your own faith in God and His Word? What would you like to see it become?

   _____

   _____

   _____

   _____

2. Read Galatians 2:16. "Justified" means you are viewed by God as if you had never sinned. What do you have to do to be justified? Are you justified by obeying the law?

   _____

   _____

   _____

   _____

3. Read Romans 14:23. This Scripture is talking about whether it is right to eat certain food. What is the truth at the end of that verse that we need to remember? What are we actually doing when we have doubt?

_____

_____

_____

_____

4. Read Hebrews 4:2. Why are some people not able to receive the message of the gospel?

_____

_____

Write out a prayer asking God to help you grow stronger in faith every time you hear or read His Word.

_____

_____

_____

_____

5. Read Ephesians 6:16. What is the importance of faith in this verse? What do you have to have faith in?

_____

_____

_____

6. Read Romans 10:17. What must you do to grow in faith? Write down your answer as a prayer, including words from these Scriptures. (For example, "Lord, I know that faith comes by...")

_____

_____

_____

_____

7. Complete the following sentences. (Answers are on page 106 in the book.)

Feeling weak, or being aware of your inabilities or limitations, does not indicate _____

_____

Feeling that God is weak toward you, or that He has limitations, is _____

_____

Read Luke 17:5. If the disciples—who were with Jesus and witnessed His miracles—made that request of Jesus, how much more so should we? Write out a prayer asking God to help you grow stronger in faith, no matter what is happening to you or how long you have to wait for your prayers to be answered. (Unanswered prayer can be a tempting reason to fall into doubt.)

_____

_____

_____

_____

_____

8. Read the following Scriptures, and next to each one answer the following question: What can be accomplished by having faith?

Luke 7:50 _____

_____

_____

Luke 8:48 _____

_____

_____

Acts 6:8 _____

_____

_____

Acts 14:9 _____

_____

_____

Acts 15:6-9 _____

_____

_____

Romans 4:20-21 _____

_____

_____

9. Read the Scriptures below, and then answer the following question: In light of this Scripture, how am I to walk?

2 Corinthians 5:7 _____

_____

1 Corinthians 16:13 _____

_____

Galatians 3:11 _____

_____

Galatians 3:13-14 _____

_____

Colossians 2:6-7 _____

_____

10. Pray out loud the prayer on pages 106-107 in the book. Then choose one of the Scriptures in the Word Power section on pages 107-108 and write it out as a prayer. (For example, "Lord, I know that the trials I am going through are an opportunity to test and refine my faith, so I pray that my faith will...")

_____

_____

_____

_____

_____

→ ←

Week Thirteen

Read Chapter 13: "Welcome God's Will and
Do It" in The Power of a Praying Life

1. Read Luke 9:23-24. What do you, as a follower of Jesus, need to
    do? Why?

    _____

    _____

    _____

    _____

2. Read Proverbs 3:6, Hebrews 10:38, and Matthew 4:10, or find
    them under "Things That Are Always the Will of God for Your
    Life" on pages 109-110 in the book. Write out a prayer asking God
    to help you do the three things in those Scriptures that are always
    His will. Be specific with each verse.

    _____

    _____

    _____

    _____

3. Read each of the Scriptures below in your Bible, or you can find
    them on page 112 in the book under the section titled "How to
    Find the Will of God." Write out a short prayer inspired by these
    verses. (For example, "Lord, I want to do Your will, so help me
    to...")

    Ephesians 6:5-6 _____

    _____

    _____

    Ephesians 5:17 _____

    _____

    _____

    Hebrews 13:20-21 _____

    _____

    _____

    Isaiah 30:21 _____

    _____

    _____

    1 Thessalonians 5:18 _____

    _____

    _____

    Hebrews 12:2 _____

    _____

    _____

4. Read Matthew 6:10. When you pray those words of the Lord's
    Prayer, you are committing yourself to obeying God, living His

way, and being willing to do what He wants you to do. Write out
a prayer asking God to help you obey Him, and do the things that
are always His will for your life.

_____

_____

_____

_____

_____

5. Read Matthew 26:39. Jesus was praying that if there were another
    way to accomplish God's will, that God would take away from
    Him this terrible path He was on. Jesus was not merely being tor-
    tured and dying; He was bearing the weight of all of our sin and
    becoming separated for a time from God. If He was willing to suf-
    fer all of that in order to do God's will, how much more should *we*
    gratefully do God's will? Write out a prayer asking God to help you
    do the specific things that are His will for you personally. If there
    are things you know God has called you to do, but you are hesi-
    tant or reluctant, ask Him to help you do them.

_____

_____

_____

_____

_____

6. Read the following Scriptures. What is the advantage in each of
    doing God's will?

    Mark 3:32-35 _____

_____

_____

Hebrews 10:36 _____

_____

_____

1 John 2:17_____

_____

_____

7. Read the following Scriptures. What is the will of God for you in each one?

1 Thessalonians 5:16-18 _____

_____

_____

1 Thessalonians 4:3-5 _____

_____

_____

Romans 12:2 _____

_____

_____

1 Peter 2:15-17_____

_____

_____

8. Read 1 Peter 4:1-2. How are we to live? Write out your answer as a

prayer asking God to help you live that way. (For example, "Lord, help me to not live in the…")

_____

_____

_____

_____

9. Most of us have had times in our lives when we did something outside of the perfect will of God. Do you ever feel you are still paying the consequences for doing something you did outside of the will of God? Or do you ever feel you are still paying the consequences for something *someone else* did outside the will of God that affected you? If you answered yes to either or both of those questions, write out a prayer asking God to redeem all of that and by His mercy set you free of every consequence. If you answered no to both of those questions, write out a prayer asking God to show you anything you may not be seeing with regard to that.

_____

_____

_____

_____

_____

Is there any place in your life now where you are concerned that you might step outside of God's will? (For example, decisions, priorities, etc.) If you said yes to that question, write out a prayer asking God to help you move into His perfect will for your life, especially with regard to that particular area. If you answered no to that question, write out a prayer asking God to show you any place in your life where you are not in His perfect will. Write down whatever He shows you.

_____

_____

_____

_____

_____

10. Pray out loud the prayer on page 115 in the book. Then choose one of the Scriptures in the Word Power section on pages 115-116 and write it out as a prayer. (For example, "Lord, help me to be filled with the knowledge of You in…")

_____

_____

_____

_____

_____

WEEK FOURTEEN

Read Chapter 14: "Recognize Your Purpose and Work
to Fulfill It" in The Power of a Praying Life

1. Read Romans 8:29. This Scripture says God knew you from the
   beginning. He knew you would exist. What has He predestined
   you to be?

   _____

   _____

   _____

2. Read Ephesians 1:15-18. What did Paul pray for the Ephesians?

   _____

   _____

   _____

   _____

   _____

Write out a prayer asking God for the same things for yourself that

Paul prayed for the Ephesians. (For example, "Lord, I pray You would give me the spirit of wisdom…")

_____

_____

_____

_____

_____

3. Read Ephesians 2:10. What does this Scripture say about you?

_____

_____

_____

4. Read 2 Peter 1:2-4. What has Christ's divine power provided for you?

_____

_____

_____

_____

5. Read Matthew 5:13-16. In light of these verses, what does God say you are? What has He purposed for you to do?

_____

_____

_____

_____

6. Read 1 Corinthians 7:7. Do you have a sense of the gifts God has put in you? Do you feel you are here for a purpose? Do you believe God has things for you to do? If you answered yes to any of these questions, explain what you believe your gifts are, what you feel your purpose is, and what you think God has called you to do. Few people know the exact answers to these questions, but they still have some inkling about their gifts, purpose, and calling. If you answered no to these three questions, write out a prayer asking God to reveal to you what your gifts are and how He has called you to use them.

_____

_____

_____

_____

_____

What kinds of things do you like to do for others? Write out a prayer asking God to use those abilities for His purposes.

_____

_____

_____

_____

_____

Write out a prayer submitting the work you do to God, and ask Him to bless it and use it for His glory. Ask Him to open up doors of opportunity for you to move into the work He has for you to do in the future.

_____

_____

_____

_____

_____

7. Read the following Scriptures. Beside each one, write what God has called us all to do.

    1 Thessalonians 2:10-12 _____

    _____

    1 Thessalonians 4:7_____

    _____

    Write out a prayer asking God to help you live a life that reflects His holiness, so that you can walk worthy of God in what He has called you to.

    _____

    _____

    _____

8. Read 2 Timothy 1:8-9. In light of these verses, what do you know about your own calling?

    _____

    _____

    _____

9. Read Romans 11:29. Have you ever thought that your gifts and

calling were uncertain, not relevant, or no longer needed? What does this verse speak to you about that?

_____

_____

_____

_____

10. Pray out loud the prayer on pages 123-124 in the book. Then choose one of the Scriptures in the Word Power section on page 124 and write it out as a prayer below. (For example, "Lord, I know that I love You and am called according to…")

_____

_____

_____

_____

Week Fifteen

Read Chapter 15: "Bask in God's Love"
in The Power of a Praying Life

1. Read Romans 8:38-39 in your Bible or on page 131 of the book. What do these verses say about God's love for you?

_____

_____

_____

_____

Do you generally sense His love for you? Explain why or why not.

_____

_____

_____

_____

2. Read Psalm 56:8-13. In light of these verses, how much does God love you?

_____

_____

_____

_____

Do you *believe* God loves you as much as is indicated in this psalm? Why or why not?

_____

_____

_____

In what way would you like your sense of God's love to improve?

_____

_____

_____

_____

3. Read 1 John 2:3-5. How is the love of God perfected in us?

_____

_____

_____

Write out a prayer asking God to help you live in obedience to His ways so He can perfect His love in you.

_____

_____

_____

_____

Read 1 John 4:18. What does the perfect love of God do for us?

_____

_____

4. Read Matthew 22:37-40. Write out a prayer asking God to help you love Him and others the way He tells you to in these verses. (For example, "Lord, help me to love You with all of my heart...")

_____

_____

_____

_____

5. Read the following Scriptures, and beside each one answer the question: Why do I love God?

    1 John 4:19_____

    _____

    Romans 5:8 _____

    _____

    Jeremiah 31:3 _____

    _____

    Zephaniah 3:17_____

    _____

6. Read Jude 1:20-21. How can we build ourselves up?

_____

_____

_____

_____

_____

7. Read 1 John 2:9-10. What happens when we love others?

_____

_____

What happens when we do not love others?

_____

_____

Read 1 John 4:7-8. What does it mean when we don't have love in our hearts?

_____

_____

_____

_____

Write out a prayer asking God to fill your heart with His love for others. Ask Him to help you pray for those you have trouble loving.

_____

_____

_____

_____

_____

8. Read the following Scriptures, and next to each one write down whom God loves.

   Proverbs 8:17 _____

   _____

   John 14:21 _____

   _____

9. How has the Lord manifested His love to us?

   John 15:13 _____

   _____

   1 John 3:16 _____

   _____

   1 John 4:9 _____

   _____

10. Pray out loud the prayer on pages 130-131 in the book. Then choose one of the Scriptures in the Word Power section on pages 131-132 and write it out as a prayer. (For example, "Lord, I thank You that nothing in life or death will ever separate me from Your love...")

    _____

    _____

    _____

    _____

    _____

→ ←

WEEK SIXTEEN

Read Chapter 16: "Put Your Hope in the
Lord" in THE POWER OF A PRAYING LIFE

1. Read Romans 8:24-25. How are we to wait for what we hope for?

    _____

    _____

    _____

    What are some of the things you wait in hope for? Are you able
    to wait in joyful anticipation that your hopes will be fulfilled, or
    are you suffering in the time of waiting? Don't be embarrassed if
    you are suffering, because many of us experience that. Peace in the
    time of waiting for our greatest hopes to be fulfilled is something
    we need to seek God for.

    _____

    _____

    _____

    _____

2. Read Romans 15:13. How can we abound in hope and be filled with joy and peace?

_____

_____

Write out a prayer about the thing you *most* hope for in your life right now. Ask God to give you the ability to persevere in hope without agony in the time of waiting. Ask Him to fill you with peace and joy by the power of the Holy Spirit.

_____

_____

_____

_____

_____

3. Read Hebrews 6:19. When we put our hope in God, what does our hope become for us?

_____

_____

Read Hebrews 10:23. Why should we hold fast to hope in the Lord and His Word?

_____

_____

4. Read the following Scriptures. Next to each one answer this question: What does God give to those who hope in Him?

Psalm 31:24 _____

_____

Psalm 33:18-19 _____

_____

Psalm 130:7 _____

_____

Psalm 146:5 _____

_____

5. Read the following Scriptures. What did the psalmist in these verses put his hope in?

Psalm 119:14 _____

_____

Psalm 119:47 _____

_____

Psalm 130:5-6 _____

_____

Write out a prayer asking God to help you put your hope solidly in His Word at all times.

_____

_____

_____

6. Read Romans 5:5. Why will we not be disappointed by putting our hope in God?

_____

_____

_____

7. What is our greatest hope mentioned in the verses below?

    1 Thessalonians 2:19 _____

    _____

    Titus 1:1-2 _____

    _____

    Titus 3:5-7 _____

    _____

8. Read Psalm 42:5. In this verse the psalmist is telling himself to take his eyes off of the situation he is in and look to God instead. Is there any situation in your life where you know you need to take your focus off of that and put it entirely on God and His Word, trusting that you have good reason to hope in the Lord and to give Him praise for that? Write out your answer as a prayer. (For example, "Lord, I confess that my focus has been on my overwhelming debt, and so I want to put my hope entirely in You and…")

    _____

    _____

    _____

    _____

    _____

9. Read Psalm 119:74. Why did the psalmist believe that people would be glad when they saw him?

    _____

    _____

Are there any people in your life who make you glad because they have hope in God and His Word? Who are they?

_____

_____

_____

_____

Write out a prayer asking God to cause people to see in you such hope in the Lord that it makes them glad.

_____

_____

_____

10. Pray out loud the prayer on page 137 in the book. Then choose one of the Scriptures in the Word Power section on pages 137-138 and write it out as a prayer. (For example, "Lord, I thank You that Your eye is always on me because I…")

_____

_____

_____

_____

_____

→ ←

Week Seventeen

Read Chapter 17: "Give God's Way—to Him and
to Others" in The Power of a Praying Life

1. Read 2 Corinthians 9:6-7. How would you describe your ability to
    give? Do you give bountifully or sparingly? Do you give because
    you have to, or because you want to? How does God want you to
    give? Write out your answers as a prayer. (For example, "Lord, I
    know I sometimes have hesitations when it comes to giving because
    I am concerned about my finances, but I know that You want me
    to…")

    _____

    _____

    _____

    _____

    _____

2. Read the following Scriptures. Write down whom you should give
    to and what happens when you do.

    Proverbs 22:9 _____

    _____

Proverbs 25:21-22 _____

_____

1 John 3:17 _____

_____

3. Read Luke 6:38. In what measure does God give to you when you give to Him? What determines how much is given back to you?

_____

_____

_____

_____

_____

4. Read the following Scriptures. What are we to give to God and why?

Psalm 29:2 _____

_____

_____

Psalm 107:8-9 _____

_____

_____

1 Thessalonians 5:18 _____

_____

_____

5. Read Matthew 10:8. This verse says that we are to freely give to others what God has given to us. The disciples saw Jesus heal and

deliver people, and He wanted them to do the same for others. What has God given to you, or done *for* you, that would allow you to bless others in the same way? (For example, "God has given me a home I could use to…" Or, "God has given me the ability to pray in faith for another person, so I could…")

_____

_____

_____

_____

_____

6. Read Matthew 19:16-26. What did the rich young man want to know? (verse 16)

_____

_____

What did Jesus tell him to do? (verses 17-19)

_____

_____

How did the rich man react to what Jesus said? (verse 20)

_____

_____

What did Jesus tell him to do in order to be perfect? (verse 21)

_____

_____

What was the young man's response to Jesus telling him how to be perfect? (verse 22)

_____

_____

What did Jesus explain to His disciples about this? (verses 23-24)

_____

_____

When the disciples asked, "Who then can be saved," what did Jesus tell them? (verses 25-26)

_____

_____

Write out a prayer asking God to help you to never put your possessions above Him.

_____

_____

_____

_____

7. Read Acts 20:35. How do we find our greatest blessings?

_____

_____

_____

Read 2 Corinthians 9:7. How are we to give?

_____

_____

_____

Read Matthew 6:1-4. How should you give?

_____

_____

_____

_____

8. Read Malachi 3:8-10. Write out a prayer asking God to help you give to Him the way He wants you to in these verses. Thank Him for the blessing of giving to Him that is listed in verse 10. (For example, "Lord, help me to never rob You by not giving tithes and offerings…")

_____

_____

_____

_____

9. Read Galatians 6:7-9. What do these verses tell you as far as giving? What happens when you give?

_____

_____

_____

_____

God asks us to test Him to see if He will bless us. He doesn't want us to rob Him of the joy of being able to pour out His blessings on us. He promises to rebuke the devourer and give us blessings so great that we cannot even contain them all. Write out a prayer of thanksgiving for the specific blessings God gives us when we sow to the Spirit in every part of our lives.

_____

_____

_____

_____

10. Pray out loud the prayer on pages 144-145 in the book. Then choose one of the Scriptures in the Word Power section on pages 145-146 and write it out as a prayer. (For example, "Lord, help me to not cling to my possessions, but rather to give generously to You and to others so that I will...")

_____

_____

_____

_____

Week Eighteen

Read Chapter 18: "Take Control of Your
Thoughts" in The Power of a Praying Life

1. Read Romans 7:21-25. Paul wanted to do good because he loved God's law, but there was another law warring within him. What was that law and what did it war against? (verse 23)

   _____

   _____

   _____

   How did he find freedom from that? (verses 24-25)

   _____

   _____

   _____

   Have you ever had a war going on in your mind that was trying to pull you away from God? Have you ever been plagued with thoughts you don't want to have? What thoughts are they? In light of these verses, how can you get free of those kinds of thoughts?

   _____

_____

_____

_____

_____

2. Have you ever had thoughts that play over and over in your mind—
    thoughts that can cause you to do something you wouldn't normally
    do (such as lose your temper or become depressed), or cause you
    to fail at something, or even cause you to feel physically ill? If you
    answered yes, write out a prayer telling God about those thoughts
    and asking Him to set you free from them. If you answered no,
    write out a prayer asking God to show you any thoughts you have
    that are not in line with the life of freedom, wholeness, and true
    success He has for you.

_____

_____

_____

_____

_____

3. Read Psalm 26:2. Have you ever believed a lie about yourself or
    your life? If so, what was it and how did you find freedom from it?
    If you have never believed a lie about yourself or your life that you
    are aware of, write out a prayer asking God to show you if there is
    anything you believe today that is false.

_____

_____

_____

_____

4. Using Eugene Peterson's wonderful paraphrase of Philippians 4:8 from *The Message*, what are some of the things you could fill your mind with that are "the best, not the worst; the beautiful, not the ugly; things to praise, not things to curse" (Philippians 4:8 MSG). Write out your answer as a prayer. (For example, "Lord, too often I imagine the worst things that could happen to me or my family or my community. Help me to instead think about the best things that could happen, such as…")

_____

_____

_____

_____

_____

5. Read Romans 12:2. What are some of the influences you see in your world that are enticing you to conform to them? (For example, images on TV or in magazines, or in your place of business or entertainment, etc.) What is your reaction to them?

_____

_____

_____

_____

In light of this Scripture, what can you do to avoid being pulled away from the will of God for your life and drawn into the enticements of the culture? Write out your answer as a prayer. Ask God to show you how to renew your mind. (For example, "Lord, help me to not be drawn toward images on television that are against what You want me to conform to, but instead…")

_____

_____

_____

_____

_____

6. Read 1 Chronicles 28:9. What kind of heart and mind did King David tell his son Solomon to serve God with? Why?

_____

_____

_____

_____

7. Read Romans 8:6. What are the two directions our mind can go in, and what is the result of each?

_____

_____

_____

Read Hebrews 8:10. What did God say He would do for the Israelites?

_____

_____

_____

Write out a prayer asking God to help you be spiritually minded. Ask Him to put His laws in your mind and heart.

_____

_____

_____

8. Read Psalm 94:11. What kind of thoughts do we naturally tend to have on our own?

_____

_____

_____

Read Proverbs 23:7. How do our thoughts affect us?

_____

_____

_____

9. Read the following Scriptures. What are we supposed to do with our thoughts?

Jeremiah 4:14 _____

_____

_____

Romans 12:3 _____

_____

_____

Colossians 3:1-2 _____

_____

_____

Philippians 2:2-3 _____

_____

_____

Read 1 Corinthians 2:16 and Philippians 2:5. What kind of mind have you been given? Write out a prayer thanking God that He has given you the mind of Christ. Tell Him what that means to you.

_____

_____

_____

_____

10. Pray out loud the prayer on pages 149-150 in the book. Then choose one of the Scriptures in the Word Power section on pages 150-151 and write it out as a prayer. (For example, "Lord, help me to keep my mind focused on You so that...")

_____

_____

_____

_____

_____

Week Nineteen

Read Chapter 19: "Refuse Negative
Emotions" in The Power of a Praying Life

1. Read page 153 and the top of page 154 in the book and write in
    your own words what wholeness is.

    _____

    _____

    _____

    _____

    _____

    In light of what you wrote, is there any place in yourself where
    you would like to see more wholeness? Write out your answer as
    a prayer. (For example, "Lord, I would like to have more peace in
    my heart about what I am doing with my life…")

    _____

    _____

    _____

_____

_____

2. Read Psalm 23:3. The restoration of your soul is important to
    God and crucial to your becoming a whole person. What areas of
    your soul do you believe need further restoration? Do you struggle
    with any negative emotions, such as anger, anxiety, fear, depression,
    loneliness, or unfulfillment? What would you like to see God do
    in your emotions? What path do you want Him to lead you on?

    _____

    _____

    _____

    _____

    _____

3. Read Proverbs 18:10. In order to enjoy emotional wholeness, we
    need the security of knowing we can turn to God anytime we feel
    weak or threatened in our emotions. Write out a prayer asking
    God to help you to remember to run to Him immediately when-
    ever any negative emotion threatens to steal your peace and over-
    take you. Be specific with any negative emotions you might face.

    _____

    _____

    _____

    _____

    _____

4. Read Isaiah 25:4. We all go through difficult times. Things hap-
    pen to us. We mistakenly do something we wish we hadn't, or the

enemy attacks us where we are most vulnerable. But God will be our strength in times of weakness. He will be our place of safety in the storms of our life. He will be our relief and refreshing when the heat is on, and our protection from the attacks of the enemy. Are you going through any kind of storm right now? Is the heat on? Do you feel weak and needy in any area of your life? Write out your answer in a prayer, and thank God that He is all the things mentioned in this Scripture. If you are not struggling with anything right now, write out a prayer asking God to help you to remember to seek Him first as your refuge from any storm that may come suddenly into your life.

_____

_____

_____

_____

_____

5. Read John 16:33. Knowing that Jesus has overcome anything you are facing, or that is upsetting to you, means there is no threat to you or your life He cannot lift you above. There is no problem or challenge He cannot carry you through. There are no emotional upsets or struggles He cannot heal. Write out a prayer telling God where your biggest challenge lies and what your greatest emotional struggle is because of it. Ask Jesus to help you live in the peace He has for you. Tell Him of the blessings you receive from this Scripture.

_____

_____

_____

_____

_____

6. Read Ephesians 2:14. God's peace is the only peace that lasts. It is the only peace that can be relied upon. It doesn't fail us. It is beyond our comprehension because it can be enjoyed in even the most difficult and upsetting of circumstances. Living in that peace is the foundation for wholeness. Do you feel you have that deep peace of God in your life? Have there been things that have happened, or you fear *might* happen, that have robbed you of your peace? Write out your answer in a prayer. Ask God to help you live in His peace no matter what happens. If you are enjoying the peace of God right now, ask God to help you to continue in that peace.

_____

_____

_____

_____

7. Read 1 John 4:16. The love of God permeating your soul does more to heal your emotions that anything else. One of the ways to open up and receive more of the love of God in your life is to thank Him for His love. Praise Him as the God of love. Write out a prayer thanking God for His love and worshipping Him as the God of love. Ask Him to help you to not only know His love with your mind, but also to experience His love overflowing in your heart. Tell Him any way you have felt unloved in the past or feel unloved now, and ask Him to redeem those places in your heart and mind.

_____

_____

_____

_____

_____

8. Read Psalm 38:6-10. In these verses, David is describing the suffering of his soul that came as a result of his unconfessed sin. Have you ever felt any of these same emotions because of guilt you felt over something you did or something you wish you would have done? Explain.

_____

_____

_____

_____

Read Psalm 139:24. Sin destroys our soul, and unconfessed sin grows like a cancer. We don't have to have robbed a bank or murdered anyone to have unconfessed sin eat at our soul. Our own unforgiveness and doubt can do that as well. Write out a prayer based on this Scripture. Ask God to show you any sin in your life. Don't feel hesitant to do that just because you are trying to the best of your ability to do everything right. We all need to ask this frequently, no matter how good we are. Sin can creep into our thoughts, words, and actions so stealthily that we don't even recognize it immediately. Or perhaps we don't *want* to acknowledge it. Ask God to show you anything in your heart you need to see. If He shows you something, confess it and receive the emotional healing He makes possible in your life.

_____

_____

_____

_____

_____

9. Read Psalm 107:8-9. What is the deepest longing of your soul? Is

there something you long for that hurts your soul to even think about? What does God say He will do for your soul? Write out these verses as a prayer, telling God the deepest longing of your soul and thanking Him specifically for all that is mentioned in these two verses. (For example, "Lord, I give thanks for Your...")

_____

_____

_____

_____

_____

10. Pray out loud the prayer on pages 157-158 in the book. Then choose one of the Scriptures in the Word Power section on pages 158-159 and write it out as a prayer. (For example, "Thank You, Lord, that You will heal me of all my emotional wounds...")

_____

_____

_____

_____

_____

WEEK TWENTY

Read Chapter 20: "Treat Your Body As Though It
Belongs to God" in THE POWER OF A PRAYING LIFE

1. Read Romans 12:1. What are you supposed to do with regard to
    your body? Write out a prayer doing what this verse asks you to do.
    (For example, "Lord, help me to always present...")

    _____

    _____

    _____

    _____

    _____

2. Read 1 Corinthians 3:16-17 in your Bible or on page 161 in the
    book. Write out a prayer asking God to help you recognize at all
    times that your body is the temple of the Holy Spirit. Ask Him
    to show you if you are ever tempted to do anything that defiles or
    destroys your body.

    _____

    _____

_____

_____

_____

3. Read Psalm 139:14. What does this verse tell you to praise God for? Do you believe that?

_____

_____

_____

How well do you take care of your body? Do you feel you need to do better in some way?

_____

_____

_____

While it is not good to be preoccupied with your body, it is very good to value it. Do you appreciate your body for all it can do, or do you criticize it for what it doesn't do as well as you would like? Are you critical of the way it looks? Do you compare your body to others and feel it falls short? Is your relationship with your body one of acceptance and appreciation or conflict and struggle? Explain.

_____

_____

_____

What changes would you like to make with regard to care for your own body? Write out your answer as a prayer, telling God how you feel about your situation and what changes you want to see happen. (For example, "Lord, I pray You would enable me to make better food choices, and I especially need Your help in avoiding…")

_____

_____

_____

_____

_____

4. Read Isaiah 32:18. How does God want His people to live?

_____

_____

Do you believe that you live that way? Why or why not?

_____

_____

_____

5. Read Isaiah 30:15. So much is lost in our lives and our health due to our busyness and the stress we are under. In this verse, God is saying to the Israelites that by returning to Him, and resting in Him and His ways, they would be saved. But they refused to do it. What can you learn from them? What can you do differently than they did?

_____

_____

_____

With Isaiah 30:15 as inspiration, write out a prayer asking God to help you find the peace He has for you so you can live stress free, even in the midst of stressful situations. Tell Him what causes you the most stress, and ask Him to help you either get completely free of it or help you find peace in the midst of it.

_____

_____

_____

_____

_____

6. Read Hebrews 4:9. What does God have for you? What are some ways you could attain more peace in your life? (For example, "I could cut back on my expenses so I would not have to work so many hours." Or, "I could make sure I spend more time with God by reading His Word and praying.")

_____

_____

_____

_____

_____

Read Psalm 4:8 and Psalm 127:2. What does God have for you?

_____

_____

_____

Read Hebrews 4:3. Who enters into the rest God has?

_____

_____

_____

7. Read 1 Corinthians 10:28. This Scripture is talking about whether
    or not to eat food that has been sacrificed to idols, but I believe it
    can also be applied to other food that is not inherently bad, but
    perhaps just not as good for you. For example, a certain food may
    be fine for other people, but not for you. Is there anything you
    know you should not eat, and yet you are often tempted to eat it?
    If so, write out a prayer asking God to be in charge of your eating
    habits and to help you to resist what you should not eat. Ask Him
    to help you crave only that which is good for your body. If you
    have no temptations like that, write out a prayer asking God to
    reveal to you anything you should not be eating. Ask Him to help
    you eat only food that is good for your body.

    _____

    _____

    _____

    _____

    _____

8. Read Proverbs 25:28. We must rule over our own spirit before we
    can rule over our body care. Is there any area of body care where
    you feel a lack of self-control, or where you would like to have

more self-control? Write out your answer as a prayer. (For example, "Lord, I don't have control over my eating habits. Help me to not overeat. Give me the ability to control the amount and portions I eat and to…")

_____

_____

_____

_____

_____

9. Read 3 John 2. Write out this Scripture as a prayer for yourself. (For example, "Lord, I pray that I will…")

_____

_____

_____

_____

Read Proverbs 12:1. Write out a prayer asking God for the knowledge you need in order to care for your body. Ask Him to help you receive any correction you need and do what you need to do.

_____

_____

_____

_____

Read Deuteronomy 30:19. Write out a prayer asking God to help you to choose life in every choice you make with regard to caring for your body. Be specific with the things that especially concern you.

_____

_____

_____

_____

10. Pray out loud the prayer on pages 166-167 in the book. Then choose one of the Scriptures in the Word Power section on page 167 and write it out as a prayer. (For example, "Lord, help me to take care of my body in a way that glorifies You…")

_____

_____

_____

_____

_____

→ ←

Week Twenty-One

Read Chapter 21: "Trust in Your Healer"
in The Power of a Praying Life

1. Read Malachi 3:6 and Hebrews 13:8 in your Bible or on page 169 in the book. If God doesn't change and Jesus is the same today as He always was, do you believe it is possible for Him to heal you? Do you believe God can do miracles of healing in your body? Explain your answer.

_____

_____

_____

_____

_____

2. Read James 5:14-15 in your Bible or on page 169 in the book. What are you to do if you are sick and need to be healed?

_____

_____

Do you find it easy to ask someone to pray for you to be healed?

Do you find it easy to pray for yourself or someone else for healing? Why or why not?

_____

_____

_____

_____

3. Read Matthew 9:20-22. What two things did the woman with the flow of blood do in order to receive healing?

_____

_____

_____

Read John 4:46-53. What did the nobleman do in order to receive healing for his son?

_____

_____

_____

Inspired by these two examples of healing, what could you likewise do in order to receive healing for yourself or someone else?

_____

_____

_____

4. Read Genesis 20:17-18. How did healing come about for Abimelech, his wife, and his female servants?

_____

_____

_____

Read Isaiah 53:5. This Scripture is talking about Jesus. How is His suffering and our healing related?

_____

_____

_____

5. Read Malachi 4:2. This Scripture is also talking about Jesus. What will He do and for whom will He do it?

_____

_____

_____

6. Read Proverbs 4:20-22. How can healing be found?

_____

_____

_____

Write out a prayer asking God to help you find healing in His Word as you read it.

_____

_____

7. Read Psalm 107:17-21. When sinful people were afflicted and close to death, what did they do? What did God do in response?

_____

_____

_____

Write out a prayer of praise to God for His goodness to heal us even when we don't deserve it.

_____

_____

_____

8. Read Isaiah 58:8. This is from the chapter in Isaiah on fasting. In light of this Scripture, what can be accomplished through prayer and fasting?

_____

_____

_____

9. Read Jeremiah 17:14. Write out a prayer to God asking Him to heal you or someone you know who needs healing. Include this Scripture in your prayer.

_____

_____

_____

_____

_____

10. Pray out loud the prayer on page 174 in the book. Then choose one of the Scriptures in the Word Power section on pages 174-175

and write it out as a prayer. (For example, "Thank You, Lord, for bearing my grief and carrying my sorrow…")

_____

_____

_____

_____

_____

WEEK TWENTY-TWO

Read Chapter 22: "Say 'No Way' to Temptation" in THE POWER OF A PRAYING LIFE

1. Read 1 Corinthians 10:12-13. What do these verses say to you about being tempted? If you are ever tempted to do something that is against God's ways, what will God do?

   _____

   _____

   _____

   _____

2. Read 1 Timothy 6:9-10. What is the source of the temptation here, and what is the result of falling into it?

   _____

   _____

   _____

   Read Romans 6:12-14. What should you do in order to not let the lust of the flesh reign in you?

   _____

_____

_____

3. Read Proverbs 1:10. What can you do to resist falling into temptation? Write out your answer as a prayer asking God to help you do that.

_____

_____

Read Hebrews 2:18. What can Jesus do for you? Why is He able to do that?

_____

_____

_____

Read John 17:14-15. Jesus is praying to God about His disciples. What did He pray that God would do for them?

_____

_____

_____

4. Read Matthew 26:41. What are you to do to avoid temptation? Why do you have to do that?

_____

_____

_____

5. Read the following Scriptures. What happens when you resist temptation?

James 1:12 _____

_____

Proverbs 28:26 _____

_____

6. Read Matthew 4:1-11. How did Jesus resist temptation? What did He do when tempted by the devil?

_____

_____

_____

7. Read the following Scriptures. What happens when you don't resist temptation?

Proverbs 11:6 _____

_____

1 Peter 2:11 _____

_____

8. Read Hebrews 4:15. Why does Jesus understand the ways you are tempted?

_____

_____

Write out a prayer telling the Lord where your greatest struggle with temptation has been. Thank Him for helping you to resist all temptation.

_____

_____

_____

_____

_____

9. Read 2 Peter 2:9. If you fall into temptation in any area of your life, what will the Lord do for you?

    _____

    _____

    Write out a prayer asking God to help you resist all temptation. Thank Him for delivering you from any temptation you are struggling with now or may struggle with in the future.

    _____

    _____

    _____

    _____

10. Pray out loud the prayer on page 182 in the book. Then choose one of the Scriptures in the Word Power section on pages 182-183 and write it out as a prayer. (For example, "Lord, I am grateful You understand how I am tempted, because You have faced even greater temptations...")

    _____

    _____

    _____

Week Twenty-Three

Read Chapter 23: "Step Out of Destructive Relationships" in The Power of a Praying Life

1. Read the following Scriptures. Write down what each one says to you about how you should treat others and how you should expect the people who are close to you to treat you, and why.

Proverbs 18:24 _____

_____

_____

Proverbs 22:24-25 _____

_____

_____

Proverbs 27:9 _____

_____

_____

Proverbs 24:21-22 _____

_____

2. Read Proverbs 12:26. We all need a sense of belonging and accep-
    tance. God wants us to have friends, but so much is said in God's
    Word about the importance of friends that we must pay close
    attention to it. What does this Scripture say about the friends you
    associate with?

    _____

    _____

    _____

    _____

    Do you feel you have chosen your close friends carefully, or are
    they haphazard relationships that just happen to you? Explain.

    _____

    _____

    _____

    _____

3. Read Proverbs 13:20. What kind of friends should you choose?
    Why?

    _____

    _____

    _____

    _____

4. Read the following Scriptures and, in light of each one, write down
    what *being* a good friend and *having* a good friend mean.

    Proverbs 17:17 _____

    _____

_____

Proverbs 27:17 _____

_____

_____

Proverbs 27:6 _____

_____

_____

Do you feel you are a good friend to others in those ways? Do you feel your close friends are supportive in those ways toward you?

_____

_____

_____

_____

5. Read Romans 12:9-13. In light of these verses, how are we to treat others?

_____

_____

_____

_____

_____

Do you feel your closest friends or family members treat you in those ways? Explain.

_____

_____

_____

_____

Write out a prayer asking God to help you be the kind of person expressed in Romans 12:9-13. (For example, "Lord, help me to continually show genuine love for my friends and family members, and to always do good to them and not evil...")

_____

_____

_____

_____

_____

Is there anyone in your life who sometimes shows a darker side of their personality to you? Explain your answer.

_____

_____

_____

_____

6. Do you have any relationship with a friend or family member who has a critical spirit? Have you ever been the object of that criticism? Explain.

_____

_____

_____

Has there been an uncomfortable relationship in the past where a critical spirit in a certain person was directed toward you? Does that still bother you today? If not, how was it resolved?

_____

_____

_____

_____

_____

Write out a prayer asking God to heal your memory of that.

_____

_____

_____

_____

Do you ever feel a critical attitude rising up in you toward someone else? If so, write out a prayer asking God to reign in the midst of that relationship. Ask Him to take away any critical attitude you may have. If you answered no, write out a prayer asking God to remove any attitude of criticism in you or tendency to be judgmental. Ask Him to help you discern when a critical spirit is in control in a relationship so you can pray that the spirit of love and acceptance will be the ruling force.

_____

_____

_____

_____

_____

7. Is there anyone in your life who makes you feel depressed, sad, hurt, fearful, hopeless, or bad about yourself? If so, is there anything you could do that might change that? Write out your answer as a prayer. (For example, "Lord, I always feel bad about myself and my life when I am around…")

_____

_____

_____

_____

Write out a prayer asking God to show you if there is anyone who feels bad when they are around *you*. This can happen without your ever meaning to hurt anyone. People can be sensitive because of things that have happened to them in their past. If God reveals anyone or any incident like that to you, write out a prayer asking Him to help you keep that from ever happening again.

_____

_____

_____

_____

8. Read Galatians 5:14. Write out a prayer asking God to help you live with this kind of love in your heart.

_____

_____

_____

_____

How hard is it to keep this commandment if someone is continually injuring you by their words or actions? God never intended for you to be harmed by someone, and especially not repeatedly. Don't be conflicted about this. Sometimes we have to let people go from our life and release them into the Lord's hands. This means if your relationship with a person does not bear good fruit, no matter how hard you try, then be willing to submit it to the Lord and ask for His will to be done in it. Write out a prayer for your most challenging relationship and release it to God. Ask God to work His perfect will in that relationship, even if it means letting go of it completely.

_____

_____

_____

_____

_____

9. If the most difficult relationship you have in your life is with your spouse, parent, or sibling, ask God to work a miracle in your heart. Ask Him to work a miracle in that person's heart as well. These are the relationships that must achieve healing and restoration in order for you to have the peace you need in your life. They are worth doing whatever it takes to make them right. They are worth praying about every day. However, you can only do so much, and you still have to release that person into God's hands. Write out a prayer for any parent, brother or sister, or spouse who is a challenge to you. If you don't have those relationships in your life, write out a prayer of protection for each one of your most significant relationships so that they always be what God wants them to be.

_____

_____

_____

_____

_____

10. Pray out loud the prayer on pages 189-190 in the book. Then choose one of the Scriptures in the Word Power section on page 190 and write it out as a prayer. (For example, "Lord, help me to know if I am contending with someone foolish who will never allow peace...")

_____

_____

_____

_____

_____

Week Twenty-Four

Read Chapter 24: "Speak Words That Bring
Life" in The Power of a Praying Life

1. Read the following verses. In light of each one, answer these questions: How powerful are the words you speak? In what way?

Proverbs 18:21 _____

_____

_____

Proverbs 10:21 _____

_____

_____

James 3:5 _____

_____

_____

James 3:6 _____

_____

_____

James 3:8 _____

_____

_____

James 3:10 _____

_____

_____

Write out a prayer, inspired by these Scriptures, asking God to help you always speak words that bring life.

_____

_____

_____

_____

_____

2. Read Proverbs 17:27-28. Have you ever said words you regret? Have you ever wished you could take your words back? Sometimes the best thing we can do is say nothing at all. According to these verses, what does a knowledgeable person need to do?

_____

_____

How can even a fool be thought of as wise?

_____

_____

Write out a prayer asking God to help you always weigh your words carefully before you speak. If you have said words you wish you could take back, confess that to God and ask Him to heal any damage that may have done. Ask Him to give you new words that will bring healing.

_____

_____

_____

_____

_____

3. Read Proverbs 11:13 and 10:18. Have you ever had someone say something bad about you behind your back? Have you ever told someone something in confidence that was of a personal nature to you, and later you found out that they had revealed that to other people? So much damage is done by those who spread gossip. According to these verses, what kind of person does that?

_____

_____

_____

Have you ever done any of those things mentioned above yourself? Regardless of your answer, write out a prayer asking God to help you avoid gossip and always keep a confidence—even if that person has not specifically asked you to do so.

_____

_____

_____

_____

_____

Read James 4:11. Write out a prayer of forgiveness for anyone who has spoken ill of you. If you have spoken ill of anyone, confess it to God and ask Him to help you to never speak ill of anyone else.

_____

_____

_____

_____

4. Read Proverbs 18:6-7 and Proverbs 29:20. What happens when we are foolish and careless with our words?

_____

_____

_____

_____

Read Matthew 12:36. What happens to us with regard to the words we speak?

_____

_____

_____

5. Read the following Scriptures. Next to each one, write down what kind of damage our words can do.

Jeremiah 9:8 _____

_____

_____

Psalm 64:2-4 _____

_____

_____

Proverbs 6:2 _____

_____

_____

Ecclesiastes 10:12-13 _____

_____

_____

6. Read Proverbs 15:1-2. What is accomplished with gentle words?

_____

_____

_____

What happens when our words are harsh?

_____

_____

_____

What happens when we speak with wisdom?

_____

_____

_____

What happens when we speak with no wisdom?

_____

_____

_____

Write out a prayer asking God to help you speak in the right way, described in these verses.

_____

_____

_____

_____

_____

7. Read Proverbs 18:13. Have you ever spoken too quickly before you heard everything the other person had to say? Has anyone ever done that to you? What can happen when we do that?

_____

_____

_____

_____

_____

8. Read Proverbs 25:11. Write out a prayer asking God to enable you to always speak words that are perfect for the person and the occasion. Ask Him to help you speak the kind of words that are described in this verse.

_____

_____

_____

_____

_____

9. Read Proverbs 10:19-20 and Ecclesiastes 5:3. Have you ever been
    around someone who talks too much? In light of these verses, it is
    clear that when we talk too much, there is a greater opportunity
    for sin. Write out a prayer asking God to help you to never talk too
    much or sin with your words.

    _____

    _____

    _____

    _____

    Read James 1:19. What are you to do slowly? What are you to
    do swiftly?

    _____

    _____

    _____

    Write out a prayer asking God to help you speak the way that is
    suggested in Proverbs 10:19-20, Ecclesiastes 5:3, and James 1:19.

    _____

    _____

    _____

    _____

    _____

10. Pray out loud the prayer on page 196 in the book. Then choose one of the Scriptures in the Word Power section on page 197 and write it out as a prayer. (For example, "Lord, I pray You will put Your words in my mouth…")

_____

_____

_____

_____

_____

WEEK TWENTY-FIVE

Read Chapter 25: "Be Holy as God Is
Holy" in THE POWER OF A PRAYING LIFE

1. Read Romans 6:17-19. What happened when we were forgiven
   and set free from sin?

   _____

   _____

   _____

   Now that we are no longer slaves of sin, what are we to present
   ourselves as? And what for?

   _____

   _____

   _____

2. What does it mean to be holy? See page 200 in the book. Can we
   make ourselves be holy or achieve it by being perfect? Explain.

   _____

   _____

_____

_____

_____

3. Read 1 Peter 2:5. What are we to become and why?

_____

_____

_____

_____

4. Read Ephesians 4:20-24. What are we supposed to do?

_____

_____

_____

5. Read Colossians 3:12. According to this Scripture, who are you?

_____

_____

What are you supposed to do?

_____

_____

6. Read Colossians 1:21-23. Why has Jesus reconciled you to God?
    (verse 22)

_____

_____

_____

_____

What do you have to do to continue on that path of holiness and blamelessness? (verse 23)

_____

_____

_____

_____

7. Read Revelation 15:4. What is the nature of God mentioned in this verse? He alone is what? How are we to respond to Him?

_____

_____

_____

Read Ephesians 5:1. What does this verse say we are to do?

_____

_____

_____

In putting these two Scriptures together, what must we become?

_____

_____

_____

8. Read 1 John 2:6. In order to become more like the Lord, you have
    to be willing to do whatever is necessary to see that happen. You
    have to decide which spirit you will align yourself with. Will you
    align yourself with the Holy Spirit of God, whom Jesus sent to be
    with you to guide you and comfort you and reveal the truth to you?
    Or will you align yourself with the spirit of darkness—the spirit
    of this world—that draws you away from all the good God has for
    you? While that appears to be an easy choice, it is not so simple
    sometimes. That's why we need the power of God enabling us to
    make the right choices every day. Write out a prayer asking God
    to help you become more like Him, and to choose Him over any-
    thing that is aligned with the spirit of darkness.

    _____

    _____

    _____

    _____

    _____

9. Read the following Scriptures. Write down what we as believers are
    supposed to do. Why?

    1 Thessalonians 4:7 _____

    _____

    _____

    Psalm 24:3-4 _____

    _____

    _____

    2 Corinthians 7:1 _____

    _____

    _____

Hebrews 12:9-10 _____

_____

_____

10. Pray out loud the prayer on page 204 in the book. Then choose one of the Scriptures in the Word Power section on pages 204-205 and write it out as a prayer. (For example, "Lord, I pray You would help me to cleanse myself and my life of anything that is filthy in Your sight, and enable me to…")

_____

_____

_____

_____

_____

> ← →

WEEK TWENTY-SIX

Read Chapter 26: "Recognize Your Enemy"
in THE POWER OF A PRAYING LIFE

1. Read the following Scriptures. Next to each one, write down what
   the enemy's plans are or what is his nature to do. In each case, what
   is another name for the enemy?

   Ephesians 2:1-2 _____

   _____

   _____

   Ephesians 6:12 _____

   _____

   _____

   2 Corinthians 11:3 _____

   _____

   _____

   Matthew 4:3 _____

   _____

   _____

Revelation 12:10 _____

_____

_____

Matthew 13:19 _____

_____

_____

2 Timothy 2:23-26 _____

_____

_____

2 Corinthians 11:14 _____

_____

_____

1 Thessalonians 3:5 _____

_____

_____

2. Some of the other names or descriptions of the enemy are adversary, deceiver, destroyer, devourer, and slanderer. Have you ever sensed the enemy of your soul attacking you in any of these ways or in the areas mentioned in the Scriptures listed in question 1? Write out your answer as a prayer to God, asking Him to destroy any attempts of the enemy to work in your life in any way. (For example, "Lord, I have sensed the adversary trying to destroy my hope and...")

_____

_____

_____

_____

_____

3. Read the following Scriptures. Write down what each speaks to you about your enemy.

   Micah 7:8 _____

   _____

   _____

   Psalm 41:11 _____

   _____

   _____

4. Read Ephesians 6:11-13. Write out a prayer inspired by these verses. (For example, "Lord, help me to put on the whole armor You have given me so that I can...")

   _____

   _____

   _____

   _____

   _____

   _____

5. Read 1 John 3:8. What is the state of someone who chooses to live in sin?

   _____

   _____

What is one of the reasons Jesus came to earth?

_____

_____

6. Read Romans 16:20. What is the promise to you in this verse? What does that mean for your life today?

_____

_____

_____

_____

7. Read John 8:42-44. In these verses, Jesus is responding to the Pharisees, who were challenging His heavenly origin. In what way were these men like the devil?

_____

_____

_____

_____

8. Read 2 Corinthians 4:3-4. Why do some people have trouble believing in Jesus?

_____

_____

_____

In light of these verses, how could you pray for someone who is filled with doubt and unbelief? Write out your answer as a prayer. (For example, "Lord, I pray You would lift the blinders from...")

_____

_____

_____

_____

_____

9. Read Romans 8:31. What does this verse mean to you? How could you use this verse if you are under enemy attack?

_____

_____

_____

_____

10. Pray out loud the prayer on pages 212-213 in the book. Then choose one of the Scriptures in the Word Power section on page 213 and write it out as a prayer. (For example, "Lord, help me to be sober and vigilant at all times so that I can...")

_____

_____

_____

_____

_____

➤ ◄

WEEK TWENTY-SEVEN

Read Chapter 27: "Fast and Pray to Win" in
THE POWER OF A PRAYING LIFE

1. Read Matthew 6:16-18. These are the words of Jesus as He taught
   a multitude of people. What did Jesus instruct the people to do
   when they fasted?

   _____

   _____

   _____

   _____

   Why do you think Jesus asked them to fast in that way? Why did
   He not want them to make a show of it? Who were they supposed
   to be doing it for?

   _____

   _____

   _____

   _____

Do you see fasting as a ritual to get over with as soon as possible, or as a part of a deepening relationship with God?

_____

_____

_____

2. In four of the many great reasons to fast in Isaiah 58:6, how would each of these reasons be especially beneficial to your life right now? They are listed below.

    "To loose the bonds of wickedness." (For example, can you think of any way the enemy is trying to establish a stronghold in your life, your marriage, your children, your work, or your thoughts? Do you see evil encroaching upon your life in any way, such as in bad language you are exposed to at work, etc?)

    _____

    _____

    _____

    _____

    "To undo the heavy burdens." (For example, are there any burdens you have been carrying on your shoulders that you have not been able to lay down, such as financial, relational, emotional, etc.?)

    _____

    _____

    _____

    _____

    "To let the oppressed go free." (For example, is there any place in your life where you feel oppressed by the enemy, such as negative thoughts, hopelessness, always feeling unworthy, etc? Do you see oppression in family members or friends?)

_____

_____

_____

_____

"And that you break every yoke." (For example, is there any place in your life where you feel you are restricted from moving on with the Lord? Are you plagued with bad memories of the past that you can't get free of, old temptations that keep coming back, or destructive habits you cannot seem to rise above?)

_____

_____

_____

_____

3. Read Psalm 35:13. In this Scripture, David had fasted for his enemies when they were sick, and they still did evil to him. What did David do when he fasted?

_____

_____

4. Read Esther 4:10-16. After an edict had gone out that would mean the Jews would be executed, Queen Esther knew she must go to the king to ask him to stop it. Why did she call a fast? What was she risking by going to the king without being summoned?

_____

_____

_____

_____

God gave Esther wisdom as to how to handle the situation, and she ended up saving her people from certain destruction. In light of what Esther accomplished through prayer and fasting, what great thing would you like to see God do in response to your own prayer and fasting? Write out your answer as a prayer to God.

_____

_____

_____

_____

_____

5. Read the following Scriptures. What happened to each prophet?

Ezra 8:21 _____

_____

_____

Daniel 9:3 _____

_____

_____

Joel 2:12-13 _____

_____

_____

Ezra 8:23 _____

_____

_____

6. Read 1 Kings 21:17-29. Ahab was an evil king, and the prophet Elijah came to him with a message from God, saying that Ahab and his family would be destroyed. What did Ahab do when he heard that message from God? (verse 27)

_____

_____

_____

What was the result of Ahab's response to God's message? (verse 29)

_____

_____

_____

7. Read Daniel 10:1-3. Daniel received a message from Gabriel about the distant future of Israel. What did Daniel do in response to it?

_____

_____

_____

Read Daniel 10:10-14. What was the result of Daniel's fasting and prayer? How long did it take for him to see an answer to his prayer? Why didn't Daniel receive an answer immediately?

_____

_____

_____

_____

8. Read Luke 2:36-38. How did Anna serve the Lord?

_____

_____

_____

Write out a prayer asking God to help you serve Him in the ways Anna did.

_____

_____

_____

_____

9. Read Jonah 3:5-10. Judgment had just been proclaimed on Nineveh for its evil deeds. What did the people of Nineveh do?

_____

_____

_____

What did God do in response to their actions?

_____

_____

_____

_____

Is there any situation you can think of in your life, or a possible situation in the future, where fasting and prayer could prevent disaster in your nation? In your community? In your family? Write out a prayer asking God to show you the things you need to specifically fast and pray about. Ask Him to enable you to do that.

_____

_____

_____

_____

_____

_____

10. Pray out loud the prayer on page 219 in the book. Then choose some of the verses from Isaiah 58:6-14 in the Word Power section on page 220 and write them out as a prayer. (For example, "Lord, help me to fast the way You want me to so that the bonds of wickedness will be loosened around me...")

_____

_____

_____

_____

_____

> ← →

Week Twenty-Eight

Read Chapter 28: "Stand Strong in Tough
Times" in The Power of a Praying Life

1. Read the following Scriptures in your Bible or on pages 226-227
   in the book. Write out a short prayer for yourself and your life
   inspired by each verse.

   Hebrews 2:1 (For example, "Lord, help me to remember to give
   heed to…") _____

   _____

   _____

   Psalm 119:161_____

   _____

   _____

   Proverbs 12:13 _____

   _____

   _____

   1 Corinthians 10:12 _____

   _____

   _____

Colossians 4:12 _____

_____

_____

Isaiah 32:8 _____

_____

_____

Proverbs 10:25 _____

_____

_____

2 Thessalonians 2:15 _____

_____

_____

2. Read Jeremiah 10:23. What do you need most when you are going through difficult times? Whom do you rely on?

_____

_____

_____

_____

3. Read 1 Peter 1:6-7. What is the purpose of certain trials you may go through?

_____

_____

_____

_____

4. Read 1 Peter 5:8-10. What happens after we have suffered a while?

    _____

    _____

    _____

5. Read Luke 21:36. What does Jesus say to do in order to escape hardships that are predicted to happen?

    _____

    _____

    _____

    _____

6. Read Proverbs 12:21. How hard is it to reconcile this Scripture with the times you have seen trouble overtaking good people? If you can think of a time in your life, or in the life of someone you know, that seemed unfairly harsh for someone good, write out a prayer asking God to help you understand His truth about the situation. Ask Him to help you not lose faith in His ability to carry you or other good people through difficulties. Ask Him to give you words to help others get through these tough times and understand how God will bring good out of it all.

    _____

    _____

    _____

    _____

    _____

7. Read Isaiah 42:16. Do you feel you are in the dark about what is

really happening in certain situations in your life? If so, write out a prayer asking God to help you to see the truth about what you are facing. Ask Him to keep you from going around in circles and always coming back to the same place. If you are not experiencing anything like that right now, write out a prayer of thanksgiving and praise to God for all that is promised to you in this verse.

_____

_____

_____

_____

_____

8. Read Psalm 37:23. There is great confidence that comes when you know you have been obeying God and walking in His will. This is especially true when tough times happen, for then you don't have to wonder if you are experiencing difficulties because you have done something wrong. Write out a prayer asking God to help you walk His way in every area of your life so that all you do pleases Him.

_____

_____

_____

_____

_____

9. Read 1 Corinthians 16:13. Write out a prayer asking God to help you do all that is suggested in this verse. (For example, "Lord, help me to be watchful in prayer and watchful of what is happening in my life and in the lives of others...")

_____

_____

_____

_____

_____

10. Pray out loud the prayer on page 226 in the book. Then choose one of the Scriptures in the Word Power section on page 227. (For example, "Lord, help me to not be shocked, anxious, or fearful when I fall into trials, but instead to...")

_____

_____

_____

_____

_____

→ ←

WEEK TWENTY-NINE

Read Chapter 29: "Move in the Power
of God" in THE POWER OF A PRAYING LIFE

1. Read Romans 1:16. What did Paul say about the gospel of Christ?
   What is it to all believers?

   _____

   _____

   _____

2. Read 1 Thessalonians 1:5. How did Paul bring the good news of
   Jesus Christ to the Thessalonians? Did he bring it in the strength
   of his own flesh?

   _____

   _____

   _____

3. Read 1 Corinthians 1:18-19. What is the message of the cross to
   those who are unsaved? What is it to those who are saved?

   _____

_____

_____

_____

4. Read 1 Corinthians 1:23-25. What did the gospel message of Christ
    being crucified mean to the Jews and the Greeks—that is, the *unbe-
    lievers*?

_____

_____

_____

What did the message of Christ crucified for our sins mean to the
Jews and Greeks who were called by God and had opened their
hearts to Him—that is, the *believers*?

_____

_____

_____

What does verse 25 say about the foolishness of God?

_____

_____

What does verse 25 say about the weakness of God?

_____

_____

Read 1 Corinthians 2:5. What should you put your faith in? What
should you *not* put your faith in?

_____

_____

_____

_____

5. Read Matthew 19:26. When Jesus told His disciples how hard it
    was for a rich man to enter the kingdom of God, they asked Him,
    "Who then can be saved?" Matthew 19:26 was His response to
    them. What does this Scripture speak to you about all God can do
    by His power?

_____

_____

_____

_____

How does this Scripture make you feel about the obstacles you face
in your life? Write out your answer as a prayer, and be specific about
what you are facing. (For example, "Lord, I still have heaviness in
my heart over what happened last year, and I fear that...")

_____

_____

_____

_____

_____

6. Read Luke 1:35. How was Jesus conceived?

_____

_____

_____

Read Luke 4:14-15. In what condition did Jesus return to Galilee after fasting for 40 days and nights and being tempted by the devil?

_____

_____

7. Read 1 Corinthians 6:14. How was Jesus raised from the dead? How will you be raised up?

_____

_____

_____

Read 2 Corinthians 13:4. What is true of Jesus? What is true of you?

_____

_____

_____

8. Read Nehemiah 1:10. How does God redeem?

_____

_____

What situation in your life do you want the power of God to redeem? Is there a specific problem you are facing right now that needs a miracle of God's power to make it right? Explain.

_____

_____

_____

_____

Write out a prayer asking God to help you move in His power in every area of your life, and specifically in the situation you just mentioned. Tell Him you depend on His power and not on your own strength.

_____

_____

_____

_____

_____

9. Read Psalm 59:16 and Psalm 145:11. In light of these verses, what should we do with regard to the power of God?

_____

_____

_____

Read Psalm 21:13, Jude 1:25, and Revelation 11:17. Write out a prayer of praise to God for His power inspired by these Scriptures. (For example, "I exalt You, Lord…")

_____

_____

_____

_____

_____

10. Pray out loud the prayer on page 233 of the book. Then choose

one of the Scriptures in the Word Power section on page 234 and write it out as a prayer. (For example, "Lord, help me to have a heart that is always loyal to You so that...")

_____

_____

_____

_____

_____

Week Thirty

Read Chapter 30: "Refuse to Give Up" in
THE POWER OF A PRAYING LIFE

1. Read 1 Peter 1:3-4. What is in these verses that encourages you to stand strong? How does this knowledge of God's Word give you faith to press on in your walk with God and in your life?

    _____

    _____

    _____

    _____

2. Read Isaiah 32:17. What in this Scripture gives you hope to keep doing what's right?

    _____

    _____

    _____

3. Read Joel 2:23-26. What in these verses gives you hope to keep going and not give up?

_____

_____

_____

_____

_____

4. Read 1 John 5:4. How can you overcome the challenges of your life?

_____

_____

_____

Write out a prayer asking God to give you the kind of faith that overcomes all obstacles. Mention specific challenges you are facing right now.

_____

_____

_____

_____

_____

5. Read Ezekiel 36:25-28. Where are the promises of God in these verses that encourage you to keep moving on in the Lord and not give up? What will God do for His people?

_____

_____

_____

_____

_____

6. Read John 14:27. Write out a prayer of thanks to God for specifi-
    cally what Jesus promises to do for you in this verse.

    _____

    _____

    _____

    _____

7. Read Colossians 3:4. Write out a prayer of thanks for what is prom-
    ised in this verse.

    _____

    _____

    _____

    Read Psalm 73:23-24. Write out a prayer of thanks to God for
    your ultimate hope in verse 24.

    _____

    _____

    _____

    Write out a prayer asking God to help you remember the certainty
    of your future. Tell God how much that certainty of being with
    Him forever means to you.

    _____

_____

_____

_____

_____

8. Read Psalm 121:1-8. What do these verses speak to your heart about all that God will do for you?

_____

_____

_____

_____

Read 1 Corinthians 2:9 and underline it in your Bible. What is the promise to you in this verse? How does this knowledge strengthen your faith to keep going and not give up?

_____

_____

_____

_____

Have you ever felt like giving up? Do you feel like giving up right now? Explain your answer.

_____

_____

_____

_____

_____

9. Read Matthew 24:13. Write out a prayer asking God to enable you to endure to the end. Ask Him to help you to never give up.

_____

_____

_____

_____

_____

10. Pray out loud the prayer on pages 239-240 in the book. Then choose one of the Scriptures in the Word Power section on pages 240-241 and write it out as a *declaration of faith* before God. (For example, "I will not lose heart, even though my outward self is…")

_____

_____

_____

_____

_____

ANSWERS TO PRAYER

What answers to prayer have you seen since you started praying
for your life? Be sure to write them down. It's important to
acknowledge what God has done and praise Him for it.

_____

_____

_____

_____

_____

_____

_____

_____

_____

_____

_____

_____

_____

_____

_____

_____

ANSWERS TO PRAYER

ANSWERS TO PRAYER

ANSWERS TO PRAYER

_____

_____

_____

_____

_____

_____

_____

_____

_____

_____

_____

_____

_____

_____

_____

_____

_____

_____

_____

_____

_____

ANSWERS TO PRAYER

_____

_____

_____

_____

_____

_____

_____

_____

_____

_____

_____

_____

_____

_____

_____

_____

_____

_____

_____

_____

_____

_____

_____

ANSWERS TO PRAYER

ANSWERS TO PRAYER

ANSWERS TO PRAYER

ANSWERS TO PRAYER

To learn more about other books by Stormie Omartian
or to read sample chapters, log on to our website:

www.harvesthousepublishers.com

HARVEST HOUSE PUBLISHERS

EUGENE, OREGON